monochrome home

monochrome home

HILARY ROBERTSON   *photography by* Pia Ulin

RYLAND PETERS & SMALL

LONDON • NEW YORK

Designer Paul Tilby
Senior Commissioning Editor Annabel Morgan
Production Manager Gordana Simakovic
Location Researcher Jess Walton
Art Director Leslie Harrington
Editorial Director Julia Charles
Publisher Cindy Richards

First published in 2015 by
Ryland Peters & Small
20–21 Jockey's Fields
London WC1R 4BW
and
341 East 116th Street
New York NY 10029

www.rylandpeters.com

ISBN: 978-1-84975-613-6

15 14 13 12 11

A CIP record for this book is available
from the British Library.

US Library of Congress Cataloging-in-
Publication data has been applied for.

Printed and bound in China

Contents

Introduction

I have an embarrassingly voracious eye; I want it all. I love colour. I love texture. I love combining both. I also believe that more or less anything can be beautiful in the right context, the right juxtaposition. And yet… as I write, I am staring at an apple green plastic laundry basket. I am wishing it were black. Or white, for then it wouldn't look so out of place in my pinky taupe bedroom.

Years of absorbing so many images, of desiring so many things, of flirting with trends and decorating fads have made me understand how helpful rigour can be. How freeing. Several decades ago, I met a girl who only dressed in black and white; some days all white, others all black, and she would also mix the two. She always looked wonderful in her self-imposed uniform; elegant, crisp, classic, like an MGM movie-star publicity shot. She stood out. And I'll bet my Farrow & Ball paint chart that getting dressed was easier for her than it ever has been for me, with my magpie approach to clothes. I'm sure she would look just as smart today. She might have changed details and silhouettes, but her no-colour edited wardrobe would always 'work'.

Scrolling through hundreds of stylish monochrome interiors on Pinterest convinced me that applying the same black and white formula to the home was an approach every bit as chic, effective and timeless as the Uniform Girl's wardrobe. Should I consider a colour cleanse? I've always veered towards large doses of white or grey but could never resist adding a dollop of turquoise, chartreuse or pale pink somewhere or other. What would it be like to eschew colour completely? How do people do that? And why do they resist the siren call of the paint chart?

OPPOSITE AND THIS PAGE Marzio Cavanna's Milan apartment combines shades of grey and numerous textural layers; linens and velvets in related neutral tones. In the living room, Marzio installed a dark metal box resembling a fireplace and painted the lower section of the wall the same colour (opposite). A black wood-burning stove in a London studio merges with the walls (left); brick painted very dark green with a top coat of black (above).

In Giorgio Deluca's classic loft, the dining area is stationed beside two graphic black metal-framed windows that become a decorative feature in such a rigorous space. Curvaceous black chairs by Norman Cherner add character and definition around the glossy white table.

After much research, I've discovered that the reasons for limiting a scheme to neutrals are almost always the same. Monochrome interiors are restful, timeless and practical. By restricting the colour palette, any number of eclectic elements can exist happily together, inexpensive or simple things look more sophisticated and decorating decisions are made easier. Creativity flourishes within the boundaries of black, white, grey and all the shades in between.

Monochromists seem to divide into two camps: those who err on the brighter side, preferring shades of white, light-flooded rooms, pale or bleached floors and a

smattering of black for details; and the others, who would happily swap day for night, veering towards darker neutrals and unafraid of the liberal use of black, creating rooms that are enveloping retreats. Both tribes understand how to shift the balance of light and dark when needed, reserving black for a bedroom or white for a kitchen, where light keeps the mood energetic rather than soporific.

Committing to a monochrome scheme might sound restrictive, but it affords the decorator considerable freedom to experiment with mixing pieces from different decades, adding pattern and layering texture. If it's all neutral, it all

works together; there's a flexibility that allows you to change your arrangements without having to wonder 'Where can I put that chartreuse upholstered chair now that my living room is turquoise?' It might take some discipline at first, but once you start editing, decisions become remarkably simple. Those hours spent contemplating paint swatches, combining them, imagining a way for all the different spaces in a home to flow visually, creating a cohesive whole are over.

There is a sub-tribe of monochromists who have not abandoned colour altogether but who opt for grey in all its variety. That might mean lilac-tinged feminine shades, a rich brownish grey the colour of dried mud and beach pebbles or a greenish sea-grey and so on. Grey is a softer, more subtle option that works best when combined in several different tones and saturations.

OPPOSITE In a historic apartment in Lyon, the contemporary kitchen is lit by an atrium. Its design is discreet and economical, with a simple white island containing storage and sink, and a bank of tall black units concealing appliances.

ABOVE The bathroom in Adriana Natcheva's monochrome mews house is covered in tiny black and white mosaic tiles, giving the minuscule room a distinctive character that continues the theme of the whole interior.

MONOCHROME
PALETTES

Choosing a monochrome interior is a minimalist stance, a refusal to get caught up in the drama of colour with all the attendant complications of what goes with what. For a monochromist, the rainbow is not an option, but there are infinite nuances of black, white and that colour in between, grey. While some elect to balance white walls with shots of black, others prefer a subtly calibrated scheme where each shade sits next to a sibling, the decorator carefully modulating the intensity used to add depth and interest. And then there are those temperamentally suited to darkness who cannot resist the striking effect of light on dark.

OPPOSITE Out of a dark backdrop, a still life emerges. Materials are key here: the gilt interior of a metal bowl, a glazed ceramic bottle in gold, a square of Dutch metal stuck to the wall behind. Darker pieces have varied surfaces too: an acorn squash, a wooden rosary, a ceramic vase and a patinated metal carafe.

In Black and White

White loves black. Black loves white. Exploiting their symbiotic relationship builds an interior that is timeless, flexible, practical and liberating. The interior that combines both black and white is greatly affected by the balance of each, the percentage of one extreme to the other. The white envelope approach (with both pale walls and floors) that wraps a space in light demands some defining characteristics if it is to be anything but a blurry snow scene. Mixing black furniture, black and white photography and a lamp or two adds punctuation to a room, and a rug combining both colours will ground it; there is something awkward about a room where objects float, offering nowhere for the eye to rest.

Given that paint companies offer so many temptingly named versions of white or black and a variety of finishes from matt to shiny, the monochromist has many choices to make: chalkboard paint is a softer black that works well with vintage and antique pieces, while gloss and lacquer suit crisper modern spaces. Brilliant whites have a more contemporary feel than softer shades, which sit well next to objects with some patina and age. Texture is all important in the monochrome interior, which relies on the tension created between hard, soft, rough and smooth to add character.

OPPOSITE A black and white scene mixes an angular white console table by Uhuru Design, a 1960s stool and a textural braided basket with a diverse group of ceramic pieces from different eras: a traditionally shaped Wedgwood vase, a layered plate by Mondays and an Eric Bonnin jug/pitcher.

PAGES 16–17 Does white equal light and black the absence of it? There is debate as to whether black and white can be called colours at all. White is defined by its lack of pigment, while black is the result of mixing all primary colours together. Each can be used in a warmer or cooler tone. Employing a mix of finishes and materials, from matt paint to glossy lacquer, will give a monochrome room depth.

Grey Matters

Welcome to the middle ground. The uninitiated might accuse the grey interior of a tendency to blandness, of being as dull as the proverbial dishwater, neither one thing nor the other, a cop-out for the undecided or those that prefer to play safe. But as every Farrow & Ball paint chart aficionado can testify, there is much more to grey than a politician's conservative flannel suit. Fashionably complex greys with names like Pigeon, Down Pipe or Plummett are far from a basic mix of black and white. The most successful execution of a grey-on-grey scheme combines several paint shades (with green, blue, brown or violet undertones) and naturally grey materials such as slate, zinc, steel or wood weathered to a shade of silver.

The *éminence grise* delights in it for its mutability; grey may be warm or cool, it plays nicely with other colours, tones down brighter shades and illuminates softer ones. It is calming and restful and, when used judiciously, far from boring. Dutch master colourist Axel Vervoordt uses the most sophisticated range of greys in the soothing interiors he designs: shades that veer towards green or brown, letting light, texture and scale operate as the decorative elements completing his sober colour schemes. In Sweden, 18th-century Gustavian interiors employed a pale blue-grey as both the backdrop and the shade used for painted furniture popular at the time, a device which produced some pared-down but atmospheric interiors that made the most of the available light.

OPPOSITE Naturally grey materials like weathered wood, patinated metal and bare branches bring textural interest to a room. A painter's canvas tarp marked with spills from many palettes breaks the rigid cube of the console table, bringing some chaos to temper all the right angles.

PAGES 20–21 A stormy sky depicted in a vintage painting is a starting point for decorating alchemy. Greys with warm brown undertones mixed with creams the colour of ironstone plates evoke a monochrome scheme that teams with rustic, raw materials like bleached wood, tweed, corduroy, natural linens, horn, pewter, rusted metal, patinated copper, weathered cedar, rattan and seagrass.

PAGES 22–23 The sophisticated use of greys combined in a graphic pattern demonstrates how effectively closely related shades combine. An interior that employs the same device — tonal variations of one colour brought together in one space — cannot help but have a soothing effect on the eye. Take inspiration from modulations found in nature: rock, sea and sky are perfect references.

Shades of Pale

There are countless good reasons to choose white. So many, in fact, that I'm baffled by people who insist on asking if I don't worry about it being cold, sterile, empty. No, no and no, I reply, quite the opposite. White is reflective, peaceful and restorative. It is the optimum choice for Scandinavians, who live in a harsh, chilly climate under leaden grey skies for much of the year. Their interiors are made for comfort not ostentation, but they have developed an extraordinary ability to create relaxed yet simultaneously sophisticated homes that put human life and its quotidian needs at the centre of design. They choose white because it maximizes the daylight that they do have and because it serves as the perfect neutral, unobtrusive canvas for their furniture and decorative objects. White and its related shades of pale seem to enlarge a space. Not only do Scandinavians like to paint their walls white, but they are also keen on cloaking floors in coats of heavier-duty white floor paint or rubbing a liming paste into wooden boards so that light bounces around from surface to surface. White isn't tricky or self-conscious; it doesn't dominate or demand attention but simply allows you to focus on living your life, to lend your character to it.

OPPOSITE White on white creates an otherworldly scene reminiscent of a Jean Cocteau movie set. White materials in clay, linen, marble, wood and plaster connect just by nature of their shared colour. Straight lines are tempered by the softness of linen folds and the roundness of the ceramic plate and marble grapes.

PAGES 26–26 A room painted white needs a combination of shades to give it dimension. Consider a palette of three different tones and vary the warmth or coolness of these; the lightest should go on the ceiling and mouldings, the darkest on the floor and the middle shade on the walls. For lustre, opt for pearlescent white paint. For a chalky effect, try unfinished white plaster.

Dark Looks

Gradually, interiors have been turning back to black, both inside and out. Black earned a bad reputation in the 1990s, when Gordon Gekko and his tribe were spending their bonuses on Le Corbusier chaises, Barcelona chairs and Artemide lamps for their newly converted loft apartments. The Matt Black era was all about acquiring the sleek, the shiny, the hard-edged; a 'lifestyle' merchandized by design emporiums for their freshly minted customers. The problem with Matt Black was its lack of imagination, nuance and texture. It was a uniform, a formula. Where was the femininity to balance all that muscular steel and leather machismo? So the archetype's appeal faded with the demise of Loadsamoney and his fat wad of cash.

Black took its time to slink back into our consciousness, but here it is, reinvented for our times in a softer, more sensual and complex incarnation. The dark materials emerging today are far more subtle, far more esoteric: ebony, Maarten Baas's scorched wood, chalkboard paint, floors made from rubber or poured resin, paint colours with names like Railings and Old Mystic, marble, slate, cashmere, suede, alpaca. A room painted in a subdued shade is imbued with a certain romance, inviting the eye to enjoy the dynamic contrast between the backdrop and the brighter things chosen as a foil. Today's dark interior is a lost continent, an island, an escape from the ordinary showcasing the extraordinary.

OPPOSITE A dark-on-dark chiaroscuro moment brings together the still life holy trinity of ceramic vessels, rusted metal and something organic in the form of a naturally monochrome leaf. The curled white edge of the sculptural leaf brings the whole arrangement instantly to life.

PAGES 30–31 Almost-blacks team together perfectly: consider shades with navy, brown or greenish undertones. Dark metals, rusted, patinated and weathered, are the ideal materials to throw into the mix.

In the Mix

A monochrome background, be it white, grey or black, demands contrast, texture and some playful elements to temper its serious side. Choosing bleached wood, a nubbly jute rug, handwoven baskets or a lampshade knitted in wool takes an interior in a modern rustic direction, whereas adding geometric copper candlesticks, a severe side chair fashioned from sleek folded metal, industrial lighting and sculptural marble objects follows a lead from contemporary Scandinavian trends. Even in the most minimal interior, accessories are the pieces of the puzzle that conjure the narrative of the person living in the space. Consider stone, a coil of rope, cast concrete, gold, zinc, black and white postcards stuck onto the wall with paper tape, a collection of curvaceous olive wood cutting boards or a group of ceramic vessels.

Compose the rough with the smooth: clean, modern elements are offset by rusticity in the form of a rattan flask, a weathered coil of rope, a hand-thrown ceramic pot, deer antlers and an off-kilter coconut shell gathered together on a vintage Belgian metal folding table.

PAGES 34–35 Copper accents in modern and graphic shapes offer a warm contrast to a dark metal vintage table. Purple green and grey sprigs of eucalyptus bring softness and subtle colour.

RIGHT In order to showcase the beautiful original details, Jonas Bjerre-Poulsen ripped out layers of 'improvements' made over many years in the life of his 1911 home. Painting the walls and woodwork white and adding the grey magnesite floor unified a diverse mixture of details, from plaster ornamentation to panelling, making the space both modern and timeless.

LET THERE BE LIGHT

Just as there are night people, there are those who prefer to bathe in light, to float on a cloud, to inhabit Hollywood's movie-set version of heaven. White can be glamorous – the pristine, impractical white on white of a starlet's boudoir (with tailored white linen slipcovers, bleached white hides, mirrored furniture, crystal chandeliers, voluminous taffeta drapes). But it can also be as unassuming and practical as a plain white T-shirt, happy to play second fiddle to whatever you combine it with, the neutral backdrop for anything and everything, setting the scene for many 'looks'. And just like its opposite, black, a white setting can have an alchemical effect on its contents, improving or enhancing whatever you combine it with; it works to *mettre en valeur*, as the French so aptly put it.

Painted top to bottom in white, even the most prosaic architecture can be transformed into a serene setting for some sculptural objects; beach pebbles, branches, tumbleweed. A basic trestle table or bentwood chair can be elevated by an all-white room. A beach hut with rough white wooden plank walls and exposed beams needs nothing more than some organic touches hauled off the shore – a weathered piece of driftwood, a large coil of rope and a pile of shells – to establish its identity.

The serene, pared-down kitchen in Jonas Bjerre-Poulsen's home is an exercise in practical minimalism, more defined by the things that have been omitted than those added. Jonas has chosen simple white painted doors for the storage cabinets floating above the floor. These are without mouldings or texture and are not fitted with any visible hardware. The work surface is made from bleached herringbone parquet reclaimed from the house renovation.

OPPOSITE The marmorino walls at Joseph Dirand's apartment have a suede effect that catches the light, changing with every fluctuation through the day. The sophisticated pale mushroom colour has been employed again in the linen that upholsters the sofa in the entrance hall, making a monochrome envelope. The cashmere blanket thrown into the mix of tactile textiles adds another subtle nuance.

ABOVE LEFT Marie Worsaae makes the most of her light-flooded attic bedroom by creating a window seat in the low window, a place to dream away an afternoon gazing at the rooftops of her historic Copenhagen neighbourhood.

ABOVE RIGHT Dark woods contrast with the dazzle of coastal light in Jonas Bjerre-Poulsen's seaside home. He prefers natural materials and claims that there are at least 100 nuances in the mix of grey and brown in his home. For Jonas, this is colourful!

Interiors stylist Annaleena Leino transformed an unpromising 1970s cottage with coats of brilliant white everywhere from ceiling to floor, adding no other colour apart from some graphic black accents, her trademark gilt-metal geometric lighting and other sinuous metallic details like the black metal hanging rails she uses to store her monochrome wardrobe (see pages 66-67). Rachel Ashwell's Shabby Chic look was founded on the idea that even the humblest piece of furniture could be improved with layers of white or pale grey paint. In the right context, white pieces from any decade will work stylishly together unified by a monochrome palette; a collection of white dining chairs from different periods can look wonderful around a table, and all sorts of upholstered armchairs or sofas can coexist happily when covered in white fabric. When the palette is restricted, a decorating scheme benefits from a variety of different styles to keep it playful and interesting.

Minimalists are often drawn to white walls and bleached floors because the pale surfaces make an ideal shell for a dramatic gesture like a large abstract painting or an architectural piece of furniture.

THIS PAGE In Marie Worsaae's home, a white
wall hung with pictures camouflages the black
screen of the television. The shiny black coffee
table is another reflective surface.

OPPOSITE The glossy black upright piano in
monochromista Annaleena Leino Karlsson's
home is both decorative object and instrument.
Annalena has found the perfect white stacking
stereo system, and even a white fire
extinguisher becomes a desirable accessory in
the monochrome scene. The floors throughout
her home are painted white, which increases
the ambient light.

OPPOSITE Joseph Dirand's soothingly decorated bedroom is deceptively simple, with creamy grey walls echoed by a bed upholstered in the same shade. Dressing the bed in white linens ensures that the light streaming into the room is maximized. Azucena sconces add a touch of metallic glamour.

THIS PAGE In the living room, on one side of the marble fireplace a substantial rectangular black desk is teamed with a Prouvé chair. There is no attempt to hide the black and white Wilson Audio loudspeakers, which resemble twin robots. An austere industrial swinging arm light is angled over the desk.

When you have decided to live with little or no clutter, the proportions of the pieces that you have selected must be exactly right or the whole space will feel awkward. Light is the essential transformative ingredient in a minimal interior.

Of course, it's natural that gallerists habitually choose white as the ideal backdrop for art. The white cube approach helps us focus on contrasting pieces. Without the distraction of competing colours, a white interior feels restful and calm, but the most successful white rooms are composed from a mixture of light, medium and dark shades in both cool and warm tones. These subtle fluctuations give a design depth. The same rules apply to the selection of objects and textures: layering different materials, from the opalescent to the matt, from woven to smooth, will save a room from blandness.

RIGHT Architect Adriana Natcheva's studio devotes much of its floor space to a glamorous kitchen/dining area, where black lacquered sliding doors conceal storage and kitchen appliances and a bar area. Adriana has used a decorative heavily veined black marble as both work surface and splashback, which makes it interesting to leave the sliding doors open.

the DARK ROOM

There is something undeniably glamorous, louche and sexy about a dark room, an atmosphere that is instantly conjured by choosing the seductive comfort of the cave. After all, it's no accident that nightclubs are habitually decorated in the darkest shades; the eye has to work harder to discover the details hidden in the shadows: a pale face, a glittering dress, a scarlet lip. Dark is mysterious but intimate. Darkness turns us in on ourselves, shutting out the world; it calms, it soothes, it envelops us in its shadowy embrace.

Going dark takes courage. Gumption. It's a commitment, and it's not for everyone. If your mood is sensitive to the amount of available daylight, you might want to limit your use of dark colours to contrasting details. Reserve the darkest shade for a ceiling, magnifying the impression of its height, or paint window frames, mouldings and doors for a graphic effect; try chalkboard paint in a hallway or kitchen, where it becomes a canvas for chalked lists or drawings and is softened by the cloudy white residue.

Darkness can have a soporific effect, so it is generally best reserved for rooms arranged for sleep or relaxation, and it's an effective way of giving a space with restricted daylight a definite identity.

OPPOSITE AND ABOVE In Maison Hand's crepuscular bedroom, the dark upholstered bed is made up with linens in indigo, marled grey and charcoal. A single red stripe adds an unexpected highlight (opposite). Ingeborg Wolf's apartment in Copenhagen devotes most square footage to white, but she reverses this in the bedroom, where both a built-in headboard and the surrounding walls are black (above).

PAGES 50–51 Marzio Cavanna's grey-on-grey bedroom combines many nuances of the shade. Hand-dyed linens have a subtle beauty, and even the accessories are an experiment in monochrome materials and textures.

Instead of struggling to lighten a dark or gloomy space, embrace the atmosphere created by going for intense, dark shades and then choose areas to illuminate with targeted lighting from lamps or candlelight.

To be successful, a monochromatically dark room demands a subtle appreciation and handling of texture, an understanding of the nuances of lighting and the skill for selecting the right contrasts and highlights. Although Maison Hand owners Pierre Emmanuel Martin and Stéphane Garotin have used several different deep, earthy colours in their 18th-century apartment in Lyon, France (see pages 90–101), the effect is monochromatic. The black painted kitchen, flooded with natural daylight from a glass atrium, opens into a chocolate brown study, which leads in turn to a khaki-tinged living room; subtle shifts that give each separate space character. Layering shades of the same intensity ensures that the scheme works as a cohesive whole yet never becomes boring. And alternating matt finishes with shiny ones and rough textures with smooth or soft ensures that there is plenty of richness here to entertain the eye.

LEFT AND OPPOSITE Accessories in metal, wood or clay are often employed as 'neutral' contrasts in the monochrome home, bringing an extra layer to entertain the eye.

ABOVE In Adriana Natcheva's studio, sliding doors open to reveal a hidden kitchen and a bar.

PAGES 54–55 Maison Hand's Stéphane and Pierre are expert at layering interesting objects and accessories that offer just enough contrast to be perceived in the dark continent that they have created in their Lyon apartment. Close examination of their preferences reveals a penchant for macabre or 'dark' elements; skulls, apothecary bottles, ravens and black glove moulds are playfully sinister decorative touches.

Ebony, slate, lacquer, concrete, metal are all dark materials that combine strikingly together. Mix those 'hard' elements with tactile and luxurious textiles – nubbly handwoven linen, buttery leather, sheepskin, mohair – and a room becomes rich with visceral contrasts that make it interesting.

As a counterpoint to the subtlety of their apartment's darkest layers, the Maison Hand collaborators have assembled collections of pale, sculptural ceramics and framed art in groups on every possible surface. These vignettes punctuate the gloom, their curvaceous and graphic shapes set in relief against the dark ground. For that is what the dark room does best: it acts as a foil for brighter decorative thing. The shiny, the sparkly, the bone pale, the lustrous – all these are required to add interest and depth.

MONOCHROME
HOMES

Monochrome interiors take many forms, from esoteric midnight black boltholes or gulag grey concrete bunkers to celestially bright seaside villas. Every decorating style may be thoroughly expressed and explored in monochrome; it's a restriction that the monochromist exploits to his or her advantage. The following case studies take us on a journey that encompasses rusticity in Sweden, cosmopolitan glamour in Milan, a studio-meets-nautical-style bachelor pad, an Asian-inflected black and white family home in Copenhagen, a classic loft in New York, a stripped-down retreat in Gotland and family friendly minimalism in Paris.

OPPOSITE Marzio Cavanna's atmospheric grey-on-grey apartment in Milan mixes five shades of grey with undertones of green, blue and brown. This corner of his living room demonstrates how using several shades and contrasting textures creates a room that feels rich and comforting.

The upper floor of Annaleena's home combines her work station, office and storage for her metalwork designs with an open-plan sitting area next to a balcony with views over the fields.

BELOW According to Annaleena, glossy painted white floors require no more maintenance than any other kind of finish. The wraparound white makes the ideal blank canvas for her brand of monochrome minimalism, which she achieves by mixing simple Ikea staples with her own designs.

RIGHT Set at an angle to the wall, Annaleena's shelves conceal or reveal depending on the angle from which they are viewed. Like many of her styling tricks, they make an abstract geometric statement.

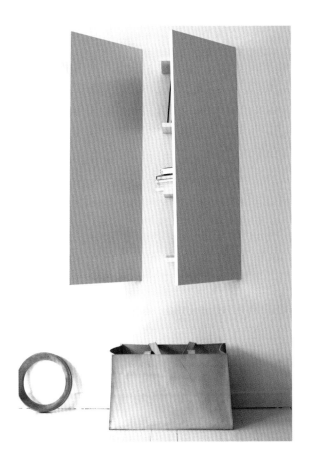

Shades of Pale

Annaleena Leino Karlsson might live in a bucolic setting, lush with electric green grass and yellow cornfields, but she makes no sartorial concessions to country living. 'Am I monochrome?' asks the ash-blonde Finn dressed head to foot in city black as she flings open the door to the white interior of the cottage she is renting while building her 'dream house' in countryside outside Stockholm. In Annaleena's universe, living in black and white is a deeply embedded reflex, as natural as breathing.

This 1950s farmhouse may be a temporary abode for Annaleena, her husband and their five children, but the interiors stylist and blogger would not consider even the briefest period of compromise or entertain another palette. A superficial makeover was required to smarten up the rental property. Annaleena's budget-friendly scheme involved laying plywood over the floors and applying lashings of white paint, disguising grotty tiles in the kitchen with panels of 'gold' sheet metal and updating the fitted cabinets with pale dove grey paint.

Two simple white leather Ikea sofas make a surprisingly practical and stylish wipe-clean seating arrangement in the living room. The round black coffee table heaped with a collection of black objects anchors the room.

LEFT AND ABOVE In order to update her rented home's kitchen, Annaleena painted all the cabinets in a pale shade of grey and had gold metal panels cut to size and fitted over the existing tiles. Her distinctly modern ceramics in pale neutrals and some shapely cutting boards are the only things out on display. The room can accommodate a rectangular wooden dining table big enough for a family of seven, flanked by vintage bentwood chairs and a bench running along the opposite side.

OPPOSITE The whiteout is complete: it engulfs every wall, door, floor and even the staircase, which demonstrates how simple architecture can be greatly improved by a paint job.

Although her 'monochromista' label comes as a surprise to her, Annaleena does wholeheartedly admit to being a minimalist. Her reasons are practical as well as aesthetic: it's just easier to keep order with less stuff, she suggests. In a household of so many children, this must be a policy conducive to sanity. Annaleena has a penchant for spare, sculptural vignettes of modern ceramics, glass and marble objects. Even utilitarian necessities like a fire extinguisher have been procured in regulation white, and the glossy black lacquer piano in the living room is quirkily accessorized with white table-tennis paddles and a cool white stereo system piled on top of it.

Annaleena's own designs – linear black metal hanging rails – punctuate the white envelope of the interior. They are a minimalist's storage solution if ever there was one, and a device that encourages the 'curation' of a tightly edited wardrobe; of course, black and white works perfectly. If anyone suggests that pure white leather sofas, walls and floors are unsuitable for children, then this family home is surely evidence to the contrary.

Annaleena's aesthetic is all about simple shapes: pyramids, squares and circles that are both functional and decorative. The black rails are put to work as a hanging system for textiles, while the folded gilt shapes may be used as bookrests.

LEFT AND ABOVE The grey master bedroom is pared down to the basics and is a lesson in how affordable minimalism can be. Crisp white bedlinen, an oversized paper globe shade and a white chest of drawers are combined with Annaleena's own black hanging rail design for her tightly edited wardrobe of monochrome clothes. Instead of art, she hangs two round gold mirrored hooks for necklaces and scarves.

OPPOSITE The upper-floor landing works as both office and sitting room, and is furnished with a convertible sofa bed upholstered in pearl grey cotton canvas. Built-in book shelves are accessorized with Annaleena's sculptural objects.

Five Shades of Grey

OPPOSITE AND ABOVE LEFT Marzio's slender kitchen table, a French dark wood picnic table found at a flea market in Milan, is teamed with white Bertoia chairs and two grey moulded Eames chairs at opposite ends. White painted panelling is scored vertically, emphasizing the height of the ceilings. Marzio has hung a collection of Astier de Villatte plates in a group on the wall. The illustrated ceramics add a whimsical decorative touch to the minimal white and grey room.

ABOVE RIGHT The apartment is full of original details, like the speckled terrazzo flooring with a black patterned fleur-de-lys border.

Some architecture has the magnetism to bewitch, the bricks-and-mortar attraction of a movie star. Milanese architect Marzio Cavanna was seduced by a grand building with a compelling amount of 'presence'. He claims he knew that he would buy the apartment before he even crossed the threshold. In the entrance hall, terrazzo floors, damask-patterned sandblasted stone walls, the grand sweep of the marble staircase and the cage elevator with its velvet banquette seat were the ingredients that convinced him that the rest would be just as beautifully conceived.

Built in the 1920s, the apartment consists of a series of rooms accessed via a 15-metre-/50-foot-long corridor that Marzio has treated as a room in itself, furnishing it with tall shelves laden with books on interiors, art and architecture, console tables and even a bench to sit on. Atmospheric lighting creates chiaroscuro moments where dramatic contrasts illuminate shapes and textures.

PAGES 70–71 In the living room, walls, mouldings and window frames painted a dark shade of charcoal grey are juxtaposed with a single black wall. The room is furnished with a mixture of comfortable classic club chairs, a rectilinear natural linen sofa, a mid-century arc floor lamp and a group of chunky wooden stools and metal plinths, which form a modular coffee table in the centre of the room.

OPPOSITE One architectural detail that the apartment was missing was a fireplace, so Marzio added a sheet metal box-like structure that acts as an essential focal point in the room, a mantelpiece for objects and vases.

RIGHT Acid green foliage, brass candlesticks and a gilded frame work as warm contrasts in the dusky gloom.

Upon entering, you are plunged into a shadowy world where five shades of dark grey paint (all of them Farrow & Ball) form the background for brighter accessories: metal floor lamps in the shape of sea urchins, sculptural table lamps, a group of stone finials and brass candlesticks.

Although it was the vernacular details of the building that impressed Marzio, his approach to decorating the space was not slavish to the period it was built in. Instead, he used the shades of grey as a starting point, painting rooms top to bottom, with mouldings, window frames, doors and skirting/baseboards all the same shade, making them instantly more modern. This sophisticated shell is layered with textures in similar hues. Antique linen curtains, alpaca blankets and upholstery in black, forest green and darkest aubergine/eggplant offer subtle relief from grey, making the space sumptuous but also calm and enveloping.

ABOVE AND RIGHT Marzio turned his hand to
making a group of monochrome pictures by
dividing an old map into three sections, framing
each one in black and hanging them together in
a row. A Saarinen table serves as a desk on one
side of the spacious bedroom. The white table,
the only light piece in this dark, deep taupe/
grey room, mixes with a tan Eames chair and a
stool upholstered in moss-coloured velvet.

OPPOSITE AND ABOVE The bedroom brings together several elements in a subtly calibrated selection of colours and textures. Marzio designed a tall, contemporary wingback headboard and upholstered it in a linen in a similar shade to the walls. The bed is made with sheets by Society in two related neutrals and a monogrammed blanket striped with black. More framed maps are hung in a vertical row on the wall, repeating the idea from the opposite side of the room.

The only space that reverses the balance of light and dark is the white fitted kitchen, where Marzio chose to profit from the natural light seeping in through elongated French windows that lead onto a small balcony where he grows herbs. As a break from the plainly painted dark walls elsewhere, he installed partial white-painted wood panels scored vertically to emphasize the height of the ceiling and mirror the style of the cabinets. A long skinny French picnic table bought at a flea market serves as a dining table and is teamed with white Bertoia chairs.

Despite the sober, masculine colour scheme the apartment is far from monastic. Marzio has pulled together the most comfortable 'man cave' imaginable by mixing hard materials with softer, tactile ones; moulded fibreglass Eames chairs teamed with a traditional upholstered sofa and club chairs, for example. And he does not shy away from the decorative, adding a gilded frame here, a curvaceous vessel there and a jolt of acidic green from the flowers he chooses, the perfect foil for all those shades of grey.

The panelled bathroom, painted in a cooler grey with blue undertones, echoes the wall treatment in the kitchen with narrow vertical grooves that give the room a clean, modern feel. Windows are fitted with shutters painted the same shade and shelves are accessorized with white objects.

OPPOSITE AND ABOVE In the monochrome living and dining room, even a deep forest green banquette sofa by Pierre Jeanneret functions as a neutral element. The polished surface of Ron Arad's Brutalist coffee table reflects the scene and ambient light. Mixing soft and hard materials and adding unexpected shades gives Joseph Dirand's minimalism subtlety and depth. The vintage black ceramic-tiled side table brings another texture and graphic pattern to the mix.

ABOVE RIGHT The heavy front door opens into a wide entrance hall with soft, suede-like marmorino walls and a deep linen-upholstered divan/box-spring sofa placed symmetrically between the two entrances to the living room.

Luxe, Calme et Volupté

Minimalists tend to be an ascetic bunch with a predilection for right angles and blank canvases, but here comes a French minimalist whose take on the most monastic decorating trope is all *luxe, calme et volupté*, a designer who prefers to create spaces that feel 'generous' and 'relaxed' however minimal they might be.

In order to fully appreciate architect Joseph Dirand's softer approach, you really need to touch, feel and brush up against the sensual combination of surfaces brought together in his Parisian apartment. The palette may be subdued, but by employing every muted shade from mouse grey to otter brown, Joseph orchestrates a stealthy assault on the senses, making these sober neutrals seem positively daring. It is the sumptuousness of all the tactile textures that transforms a symphony in greige into a svelte retreat calibrated for the subtlest of sybarites.

ABOVE AND RIGHT The 'breakfast nook' in the sleek yet practical kitchen is not only a perfectly composed mix of vintage and modern but also a useful informal space for family dining. Thick slabs of marble and glossy polished wood cabinets add glamour to the work space. Positioning the fitted storage on the opposite side of the room means that the deep shelf above can be devoted to both decorative and meaningful objects, such as the photograph by François Halard.

Such restraint works when architectural details are as crisp and well executed as these: walls finished in marmorino plaster, a finish composed of marble dust and lime putty that takes on the appearance of suede; herringbone *parquet de Versailles*, floors bleached to a shade of pale that's more typically Scandinavian than Gallic; floor-to-ceiling French windows fitted with plainly painted off-white shutters. The *grand luxe* finishes extend to kitchen and bathrooms gussied up with vast chunks of paonazzetto marble. The space gives the impression of architectural authenticity, but history has been reinvented here. As he couldn't find an apartment with vernacular details intact, Joseph commissioned them to

LEFT Joseph Dirand's Paris apartment marries 21st-century minimalism with details from the past. The living room brings together favourite pieces of furniture by Pierre Jeanneret upholstered in forest green suede, an abstract painting by Lawrence Carroll and a coffee table by Ron Arad.

ABOVE Playing with several materials in related shades, Joseph covered the sofa in the entrance hall in linen in a deeper shade of taupe than the walls and added a fringed throw in a paler shade, one more layer of luxurious texture enhancing the muted palette.

be made from scratch: bronze door furniture and plaster mouldings inspired by 17th-century Italian buildings rather than Haussmann's decorative Parisian embellishments.

It's hard to imagine a Parisian as chic as Joseph Dirand referring to anything as a 'breakfast nook', but the kitchen is large enough to accommodate one of these practical arrangements, with a vintage table by Ettore Sottsass and an upholstered banquette teamed with two Prouvé chairs. Tall cupboards conceal the usual kitchenalia, but a long marble shelf along the 'working' side of the room allows a rare moment of display, collecting together vases, glass decanters and a framed photograph by family friend François Halard.

RIGHT At one end of the combined living/dining room, a massive wooden dining table teamed with Pierre Jeanneret masculine square-backed dining chairs takes the palette to a darker place. Two intricate mid-century gold pendant hanging lights are slung low over the table. The symmetry of the arrangement echoes the architecture of the room, with its two entrances from the hall.

OPPOSITE AND ABOVE The tranquil, bone-white master bedroom, with its marmorino walls and crisp painted woodwork, is furnished with a few sculptural mid-century pieces including an Oscar Niemeyer suede-covered chair and footstool, and wall sconces by Italian lighting company Azucena.

RIGHT In the bathroom, the walls are clad in giant slabs of dramatically veined marble. More marble forms an innovative sink unit, where water drains away via a discreet horizontal slot.

The architect's taste in furnishings involves many desirable design classics: in the living room there are angular chairs and a sofa by Pierre Jeanneret, a Brutalist metal coffee table by Ron Arad, a Corbusier table and then the anomaly, a sprawling, squashy Living Divani linen sofa strewn with cushions. 'Accessorizing' may be antithetical to the minimalist state of mind, but Joseph Dirand has allowed flashes of primary colour to make their way into the scheme in the form of an abstract painting by Lawrence Carroll, a red platter by Sterling Ruby, ceramic vases in an acid yellow and a collection of books with graphic covers; playful touches that strike a less serious note. If anyone can make minimalism simultaneously livable and sexy, it's Joseph Dirand.

Round Midnight

Serial renovators Pierre Emmanuel Martin and Stéphane Garotin, both
dedicated 'monochromistes', preside over a sophisticated decorating empire
based in Lyon in the South of France. Their store Maison Hand is the go-to
destination for the chicest of Euro-luxe interior merchandise; an intoxicating
mix of rough with smooth, of rusticity blended with opulence. Naturally, their
own homes have been put to work as laboratories for new ideas and products.
Barely a year or so ago, they discovered this 16th-century building near the
Saône River in the heart of Old Lyon, just five minutes walk from the shop.

A warren of rooms, gloomy and covered with exposed electrical wiring, the
interior required a drastic approach and a singular vision; it was the sort of project
that professionals approach with relish. Partition walls were demolished, creating
a 50-square-metre/538-square-foot living space that runs on an axis from the
front elevation to the back. The glass atrium added at one end created the ideal
space for a new kitchen; essential to Stéphane, who likes to cook for a crowd.

The black and white kitchen is lit by natural light from an atrium, so despite the glossy black tiles and bitter chocolate walls, the space is bright. A white island conceals storage and houses a sink and hob/stovetop. The part-tiled wall is built out enough to include a shallow shelf for utensils, chopping boards, bottles of olive oil, African baskets and a black anglepoise lamp.

ABOVE AND RIGHT The blue velvet sofa (the Mustique by Gordon Guillaumier) makes an interesting contrast with the chocolate walls. The Noguchi glass-topped coffee table sits on a Berber rug. The black metal floor lamp is the AJ by Arne Jacobsen.

The layout that emerged is dynamic; one room flows into the next and the absence of doors allows tempting glimpses of what lies beyond. Obviously, the enfilade of rooms required a colour palette that flowed just as seamlessly, a combination of related shades that would work for the entire space.

As their last apartment was an exploration of white on white, here Pierre Emmanuel and Stéphane decided to experiment with the other side of the prism, plunging enthusiastically into new territory where shades of deepest coal, blackened khaki and midnight indigo rub up against each other.

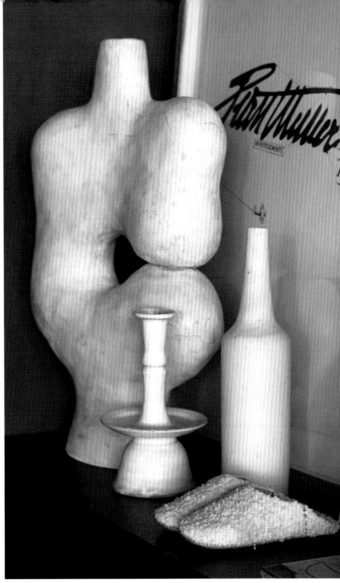

LEFT AND ABOVE A long rosewood sideboard is laden with multiple vignettes of framed art, lamps in different styles, ceramic sculptures and small ceramic bowls all in shades of white and parchment, which look all the more intriguing against the background. A white Saarinen marble-topped table is another shape standing out against the dark background.

PAGES 98–99 A hefty, square, black-stained wooden table makes an unusual but satisfyingly solid shape in the dining area, where the pale woven rush seats of the accompanying black-framed dining chairs help to define the space by their bright contrast. A group of black and amber ceramic cylinder vessels, plain or with coordinating surface patterns and of different heights, makes a bold modular centrepiece on the dining table.

ABOVE AND OPPOSITE On an upper floor overlooking the courtyard garden, the charcoal grey bedroom is an intimate retreat tucked away from the public spaces. A large upholstered bed layered with pale grey, indigo and bone linens is orientated towards the view, and the master bathroom, just visible through an open doorway, conceals a wet room tiled from top to bottom. The pale Berber rug bounces ambient light from the French window, and a vintage brown leather Eames lounger stationed next to the window looks back into the room. An oversized mirror leaning against the wall brings an extra dimension to the interior. Framing art in white focuses attention on the imagery.

Experts in creating vignettes, they have layered contrasting accessories, found objects, ceramics and piles of books in shades of bone, cream and linen that look all the more sculptural in relief against the dark background. These arrangements seem to float in space, a virtuoso demonstration of chiaroscuro.

In this realm of darkness, all sorts of lighting (apart from overhead) plays a vital role, highlighting collections or areas arranged for reading or dining. Tactile textures – velvet, leather, wood and marble – give the scheme depth, as do subtle contrasts like the navy velvet sofa teamed with dip-dyed linen curtains and natural wool Moroccan rugs against the chocolate-stained walnut floors. The Maison Hand look is simultaneously understated and complex, referencing many of the places that they like to travel to in search of handmade pieces: baskets from South East Asia, statues from Indonesia, cushions from Thailand. At night the dark interior, a cosy retreat for the senses, has an other-worldly quality that Pierre Emmanuel and Stéphane find magical and relaxing.

Dark and Stormy

The Swedes have a rhythm to their year that's determined by extremes of light and dark. After months of dark afternoons and endless nights, they seize long summer days with gusto, milking every golden moment from the season. Stockholm is surrounded by islands that are easily accessed by boat or ferry, so many city dwellers keep a *sommerhus* in the archipelago, a weekend or holiday escape that allows them to live close to nature for those precious warm months.

Architects Henrik and Lotta Imberg have created a back-to-nature getaway beside the Baltic Sea on Furillen, just off the island of Gotland. In the spirit of 'green' architecture, the Imbergs decided not to build a new structure but instead rescued an abandoned garage built circa 1961 to hold military vehicles. It was near collapse, but they saw potential in the large wooden shed with its sloping roof and doors opening onto a wild plot of land, oriented towards sky and sea.

The interior has been divided up by stud walls that screen off different zones but still allow views from end to end. The largest area is a dining/cooking space, with a long dining table in front of a wall of windows and doors to the outside.

OPPOSITE Although many interior walls were left as raw plywood, the Imbergs have used several paint colours to define different areas. A dividing wall painted grey separates the entrance area from the kitchen. The same shade of dark slate covers tall freestanding cupboards that hold tableware and other kitchenalia.

ABOVE LEFT Nothing is precious in this summerhouse: rough, unpainted shelves hold books and homemade accessories. The Imbergs experimented with casting decorative objects from poured concrete; these bookends take their shape from plastic mineral water bottles.

ABOVE RIGHT Even the refrigerator doors have been painted the same shade of steely grey, integrating it into the colour scheme.

The middle section of the structure is occupied
by a utilitarian but supremely practical kitchen
– just a hot plate, a dishwasher and a white-
tiled splashback – while the long dining table is
stationed opposite doors that open directly to
the outside and views of the sea and forest.

LEFT The indoor living area is an ad hoc arrangement of some vintage pieces inherited from parents, outdoor furniture and basic pieces purpose-made for the space, like the rough-hewn day bed. The fern-printed fabric on the 1940s chair is the one unexpected hit of pattern in the whole arrangement. Two white metal garden tables serve as occasional tables.

ABOVE Low white metal trestles combined with wooden planks make a low sideboard used for holding books and a lamp.

The whole of this elevation of the shed opens onto a wild outdoor view of pine forest, rocks and sea, making this the ideal spot for dining whatever the weather. Chairs are softened by monochrome sheepskins sourced locally.

OPPOSITE The Imbergs refinished the concrete shuttering, which is taken up to dado height, but left the rest of the walls as raw plywood. The children's bedroom is decorated with a shade of cobalt blue on the bunk bed and chest of drawers, yet monochrome accessories like the paper lantern collaged with newsprint and small framed prints keep the theme going.

LEFT A canvas teepee creates a room within a room and can be moved outside in the blink of an eye.

BELOW The monastically simple main bedroom is as pared down as possible, with a white mosquito net suspended above a low mattress. A plain navy blue bedspread matches the painted wall and natural canvas curtains conceal storage for clothes.

A functional but basic kitchen was built along the back wall. The next section is a sitting area furnished with mid-century armchairs and a day bed, vintage pieces found locally or inherited from grandparents. At the furthest end are two minimalist bedrooms.

In keeping with the utilitarian style of the shed's structure, furniture and fittings are pared down and the materials used are raw and neutral in colour. The original grey concrete floor is practical for the indoor/outdoor life; marine ply walls have been left unfinished or painted greyish shades of steel blue or sage green inspired by the landscape beyond. Henrik and Lotta now plan to 'winterize' their home, making it possible to visit year round.

OPPOSITE AND THIS PAGE

The ground floor comprises two large rooms: a kitchen and a dining room. Floors are made from poured concrete and the thick walls are plastered in a rough grey render similar in tone to the smoother floor.

PAGES 114–115 A magenta abstract painting and a wooden sliding barn door distract from the grey bunker Brutalist dining area, while locally sourced sheepskins flung over the chairs add a welcome note of softness.

The Concrete and the Clay

Surrounded by rock, sea and sky, Johan Israelson's home on Gotland, an island in the Stockholm archipelago, seems to have evolved in response to its surroundings. It's as rough and elemental as the sedimentary rock it was built on. Inside the weathered cedar exterior, grey walls and poured concrete floors conjure up the architect's 21st-century version of rusticity.

Johan's love affair with the most basic building material has led him to experiment with concrete in many forms. It provides the textural shell of the structure and is used to create everything from the kitchen work surfaces to bathtubs and sinks, while a mighty slab of it forms the dining table. Anyone with an aversion to the medium or to neo-Brutalist architecture in general might find the sheer amount of it overwhelming, but in this rustic modern context its no-colour colour and its mutability as a material (it can be rough, polished smooth or imprinted with pattern) establishes a sophisticated mood that's perfectly suited to the terrain.

The floorplan of the main house devotes the majority of the ground floor to a large dining room and kitchen, but there is also a small sunny den where plants thrive and a deep window seat, strewn with cushions, offers a cosy escape from the rigour of the public spaces. Upstairs, a loft-like space that stretches over the whole footprint of the house and opens to the roof beams makes the ideal recreation room for family life; a sparsely furnished multi-purpose home to computers, television and all the equipment necessary for indoor entertainment when the weather prevents alfresco living.

Many Stockholmers use the island as a weekend escape, but the Israelsons live here all year round.

LEFT AND ABOVE The kitchen continues the concrete theme, with a work surface and shelf cast from the stuff. A painted wooden ceiling and stainless-steel appliances provide contrast.

PAGES 118–119 In the bucolic compound consisting of several separate structures, this rough, unpainted wooden shed is devoted to summer dining and has its own kitchen at one end.

They have fashioned their rural plot into a U-shaped compound
that's designed to blur the boundaries between inside and out.
Apart from the main house, there is a collection of outbuildings:
a guest cottage, a garage for storage and a large wooden shed that
houses another kitchen and a huge dining table ideal for summer
gatherings. Both the shed and the main house have attached
outdoor seating areas; one incorporates built-in benches and a fire
pit for warmth and outdoor grilling, and the other provides yet
another open-air living room furnished with table, chairs and day
beds that's perfect for entertaining. The naturally monochrome
materials used for every structure complement rather than
compete with the landscape.

Contributing to the impression of a self-sufficient rural idyll,
there is a free-range white Angora rabbit skittering around the
house, a paddock for goats and a vegetable garden with neatly
organized square beds that have been framed in the same
weathered wood used throughout the project.

OPPOSITE Throughout the house, Johan Israelson has experimented with concrete in all its forms, creating a cast-concrete top for the dining table, a cast-concrete sink in the bathroom and even a bathtub made from the material.

THIS PAGE A spacious upper floor exposed to the eaves houses a simply furnished master bedroom and a recreation room.

OPPOSITE AND THIS PAGE Naja Munthe, a fashion designer known for her textiles, has produced several large abstract canvases for her home. The rough-hewn stool (opposite) is typical of her taste: a sculptural form in black that shares the DNA of the textural painting. The children's bedroom shares the same palette as the rest of the apartment (above right).

PAGES 124–125 Naja has lived in the apartment for 13 years but is still making adjustments. She added two symmetrical metal-framed windows that divide the entrance hall from the living room. Below these are two banquettes topped with the softest buttoned suede cushions.

Perfectly Balanced

If ever a nation's identity was bound up with a very particular sense of interior style, it is Denmark's. Danes are deservedly proud of their design heritage: Wegner, Jacobsen, Juhl et al have all contributed classic pieces of furniture as comfortable as they are stylish to the design canon. The notion that style and comfort should go hand in hand is the mantra of the Danish home, the very thing that separates it from those interiors schemes made just to be admired, that demonstrate how ably the owner can explore a theme rather than cater to how people actually live or the exigencies of family life. The Danish home is arranged to be a place to relax, work, cook or play, not as a visual experiment with the creative uses of fringing or moire velvet. It can be quite plain; in fact more often than not it is delightfully plain and simultaneously sophisticated, and of course the whole is very likely to be executed in monochrome.

A whole room is devoted to Naja's minimal
home office; a mid-century desk floats in the
middle of the space between windows onto the
garden. She keeps inspirational objects from her
life and travels here: a stone bust, a collection
of paintbrushes, an Eastern deity and a tiny
pair of vintage baby shoes.

Fashion designer Naja Munthe claims she can open any interiors magazine and instantly tell a Danish home from even a Swedish or Norwegian one, so embedded and homogenous is the aesthetic she grew up with. Her apartment in a sprawling 1864 villa in the centre of Copenhagen is a case in point. It boasts all sorts of original 19th-century architectural details that give the interior character – a white ceramic *pejs* (stove), herringbone parquet floors and tall windows – but the feel she has imbued it with is distinctly modern and eclectic.

ABOVE LEFT Naja has two adjacent bathrooms, one fitted with a soaking tub and the other a practical wet room next to the master bedroom. This is tiled in black slate with white painted walls and deep storage drawers under the sink.

Naja suggests that her preference for a monochrome scheme allows her to experiment with mixing diverse accessories, art and furniture without the whole becoming a confusing ragbag of different influences. Her Asian, Indian and Japanese pieces add an unexpected layer of exoticism to the overall theme of comfortable, practical Danish simplicity. And as she likes to change and rearrange constantly, sticking to the neutral colour palette makes it possible for everything Naja owns to work in every context.

ABOVE The custom in Scandinavia is for couples to sleep under separate duvets, so Naja makes up the bed with neatly folded piles of coordinating linens and pillows. The black wood custom-built headboard with cubbyholes for books and accessories is a recent addition and an alternative to bedside tables.

Night Owl

Penetrating the crepuscular gloom of Parashkev Nachev's London mews house, you could be forgiven for thinking that you had strayed into the city's latest underground *boîte*. All is inky black paint, reflective lacquer finishes teamed with sparkly copper details and vintage leather club chairs. A neuroscientist and neurologist by profession but amateur product designer by night, Parashkev decided that, as he was unlikely to spend many daylight hours in his diminutive home, he would embrace the 'dark side' and opt for a colour scheme that comes into its own after dusk. Midnight black walls and dark stained wooden floors are a dramatic backdrop for some inventive decorative details, not least a giant coil of rope artfully heaped on the mezzanine's balustrade.

When he arrived here, the floor plan was awkward and the light limited to north-facing windows on one side only, so Parashkev commissioned his sister,

OPPOSITE AND THIS PAGE The ceiling in the studio, a perfect square, is painted metallic bronze, reflecting light from the huge sash window at the front of the space. The brick walls have been painted a greenish black and the floor is ebony. The large circle of copper on the wall is a light fixture designed and made by Parashkev. The black Perspex desk with bronze legs is also his own design.

ABOVE A wall of black shelves covers one side of the sitting room and houses books, records, a stereo system and materials for DIY projects.

RIGHT A woodpile next to the black iron wood-burning stove works as a texture break in the plainly painted space. A double-ended leather chaise and two leather armchairs form a sitting area in front of black Plexiglass doors, which conceal clothes storage and a utility room.

PAGES 134–135 Natural materials – burnished leather, coiled rope, glass and metal – stand out as if in relief against the black backdrop.

architect Adriana Natcheva, to re-imagine the space using every square inch to advantage. With its economical layout – a space-saving platform bed, ingenious storage areas tucked into every nook and cranny and a neat little kitchen – the place has much in common with a boat, albeit one envisioned by a stylish vampire.

Adriana installed a large window at the front of the studio complete with mahogany shutters for privacy and added windows at the back. The black lacquer sliding doors opposite the window conceal the closet and also allow space for the more mundane workings of a home: washing machine, linen storage and so on. However, most of the

floor plan is devoted to a generously proportioned living space, a perfect 5 x 5-metre/16.5 x 16.5-foot cube with a very simple but theatrical colour scheme of dark greenish black walls, a bronze ceiling reflecting light from the large window and wooden floors combined with warm accents of leather and copper – the perfect foil for the darkness.

After hours, Parashkev likes nothing better than a creative project – designing his own light fixtures or illustrating a book of his favourite recipes; his inventiveness is boundless. He even encouraged his girlfriend to spend her evenings fashioning a rope ottoman from a car tyre and a length of rope, apparently a very time-consuming pursuit.

OPPOSITE AND ABOVE A tiny eat-in kitchen reminiscent of a ship's galley is tucked into a space at the back of the mews house. Two vintage machinist's stools and a burnished wood surface fixed to the wall function as a dining area. The same grainy wood finish is used for the splashback and work surface

RIGHT As diminutive and pared down as a ship's cabin, the bedroom on the mezzanine is just big enough for a mattress and concealed cubbyhole storage in the floor.

Light Touch

OPPOSITE Just a few telltale signs reveal that this is an eight-year-old boy's bedroom, albeit a very sophisticated one. The divan/box spring bed is made up with cosy blankets and knitted cushions in a mixture of dark shades. Two low tables can be put to use as surfaces for play.

ABOVE When Jonas bought it, the 1911 house had been extended twice and had seven different layers of flooring. While the design was well integrated from the outside, it was confused on the inside where various former owners had added to a patchwork of styles. Jonas took up all the floors, levelled them and cast a magnesite floor to provide contrast with the ornamented walls and ceilings.

Jonas Bjerre-Poulsen does everything: a partner in Copenhagen-based practice Norm, he juggles several interconnected careers as architect, product designer, stylist and photographer, imagining and capturing serenely monochrome interiors and the pieces that fill them. Perhaps sensibly for such a busy man, he chooses to live not in the centre of Copenhagen but rather in a spacious 19th-century house in a sleepy, well-heeled coastal suburb about 40 minutes away.

As a contrast to a life of creative multi-tasking, his family home is as pared down as his days are full; soothingly minimal and palette-cleansingly empty of anything that might distract from the exquisite bones of this grand Arts and Crafts villa, with its high ceilings, panelled walls, curved bay windows and stone fireplaces. His own understated designs for furniture, lighting and ceramics work perfectly to complement the original details without overwhelming them. Painting all the walls in matt white and covering the original floors in polished concrete adds a layer of 21st-century cool, subtly updating the atmosphere. The many windows are bare of curtains or blinds but texture is added in the form of textiles in subtly related shades of charcoal, cocoa, grey and black.

OPPOSITE AND BELOW The dining room is furnished with pieces designed by Jonas and that embody his philosophy; well-crafted furniture with clean and modern lines reminiscent of Scandinavian classics, pieces that might be handed down from generation to generation. According to Jonas, minimalism is not a modern style but has been the norm in many cultures since the beginning of civilization: 'Reduction and perfection have been the main goal for both craftsmen and inventors – because avoiding the irrelevant means emphasizing the important.'

ABOVE In the hallway, a severe rectilinear black wooden side chair sits below two modern wooden ledges used as places to lean a photo or small object. This is an alternative approach to hanging framed pictures, which cannot be swapped around as easily.

THIS PAGE The kitchen was renovated in contemporary style, but Jonas reused materials from the old house; the original herringbone flooring became the kitchen work surface, for example. This tranquil room epitomizes the stripped-down simplicity that Jonas aims for in all his designs.

OPPOSITE As some spaces were dark, Jonas cut niches in the walls to allow daylight to travel through. The lamp is one of his own designs.

A room between the kitchen and the living room is used as an office, with a large pinboard plastered with postcards, magazine tears and photographs covering one wall and a desk placed centrally. A metal shelf unit with square cubbyholes holds an assortment of books and accessories.

THIS PAGE The sleek magnesite flooring and white walls throughout provide a calm, understated backdrop to the Neoclassical and Art Nouveau architectural detailing and embellishments.

OPPOSITE The master bedroom is in an extended wing of the house, accessed by a shallow staircase added by Jonas. The serene space has very little in the way of decoration, but what it lacks in accessories it makes up for in architecture, with large windows and a vast curved fitted armoire that wraps around a corner of the room, providing essential storage.

The kitchen is a model of discreet modernism, with its back-to-basics gas stove mounted on four slim metal legs. There are no wall units, just a stretch of white cabinets topped by a wood work surface along one wall, and the space is punctuated by bare lightbulbs hung low on long, twisted cord cables. To compensate for the monastic plainness, there are vignettes of carefully chosen utilitarian objects like the sculptural chopping boards in one corner and the clutch of ceramic vessels on the windowsill.

Such rigour might seem antithetical to family life, but one imagines that such a soothing arrangement of space encourages the development of equally serene human beings who put away toys and don't scribble on walls. Minimalism demands plenty of storage space to conceal all the clutter of everyday life, and that inhabitants are disciplined about maintaining order. It must help that just a few metres away there's a strip of sandy beach to play on and the bracing Øresund to leap into during the summer months.

THIS PAGE AND OPPOSITE
The living space in this carriage house is accessed via a staircase from the entrance hall on ground level, so it sits higher than most living quarters, making it very light. The kitchen takes up half the footprint of this area and is big enough for a large oak dining table and comfortable chairs.

Sweetness and Light

Do the Danes have something against colour? Is there some unwritten national code that insists on the exclusive use of sober neutrals? If you read Scandinavian interiors magazines, you might assume that they do and there is, so rampant is the Nordic trend for monochrome.

Marie Worsaae is no exception, with a home conforming strictly to code. Her bijou one-bedroom listed carriage house in a quiet cobbled courtyard in the centre of Copenhagen is black and white both inside and out. Marie found her home through a friend who had lived there and, after two years, she is still enchanted by its history and character. Once an artist's studio, it is believed that the great Danish painter Vilhelm Hammershøi worked here (a prime example of the Danish devotion to greyscale, the painter used only the most muted shades of grey, white and black to evoke atmospheric 19th-century interiors and architecture). Naturally for a building used as a studio, the space is flooded with light from the vast window in the living room, skylights in the attic bedroom and a round window in the façade. The open-plan layout on the ground floor means that Marie feels she is living 'in the whole space at one time'.

As for the Danes' default setting for decorating in monochrome, Marie explains that it relates to a desire for spaces that offer a soothing retreat from the outside world without the 'confusion or distraction' of colour. It's not just her home that is monochrome. Marie is the owner of Aiayu, a business that makes clothes and home accessories from Bolivian llama wool.

In the kitchen, dark wood cabinets run along one wall and there are no wall cabinets. Instead, a long black shelf is used as an opportunity to display pictures and objects. A group of olive wood chopping boards on the work surface add a welcome organic touch.

ABOVE A tall, glazed black vitrine stores glassware and ceramics in neutrals and pale pastel colours.

RIGHT There are so many charming original features here that Marie found furnishing the apartment straightforward and used many pieces from her last home. She did invest in a squashy, linen-covered Verzelloni L-shaped sofa, which is scattered with soft alpaca cushions from her Aiayu range. The whole of the wall opposite is devoted to a collection of prints and paintings hung salon style.

THIS PAGE AND OPPOSITE The upper floor in the eaves of the building is divided by a small box room housing a bathroom. Marie loves to lie in bed listening to the rain on the skylight or sit on the low window ledge. A desk butts up against the staircase balustrade, where she has gathered a collection of shells and stones.

She creates new products every year but always sticks to a core palette of neutrals, from the palest shade of cloud grey to the darkest charcoal (the llamas who provide the wool have coats in 13 natural colours), and every season she adds some subtle dyed shades as accents. She admits that her last home had a very similar feel and she transferred many pieces from there. However, the scale of this space allowed for the addition of a generously proportioned L-shaped grey linen sofa that's heaped with woollen cushions and blankets from the Aiayu collection. In the living room, a whole wall, almost 4 metres/ 13 feet high, is devoted to a group of monochrome-framed art hung salon style, and a painted black vitrine houses vintage glasses, plates and vases; everyday pieces that are both decorative and useful. The softest pastel accent colours – lemon yellow, pale pink and eau de nil – recur in the mix, a subtle dose of femininity that destabilizes the masculinity of the reigning monochrome scheme.

Perhaps Hammershøi's quietly brooding paintings provide a vital clue to the Nordic rejection of colour. In his interiors, the grey rooms are bare of decoration. Instead, drama and beauty comes from the way he is able to depict light falling. Winters in this region are long, chilly and dark, so the subtleties of light are appreciated more than any man-made decorative flourishes. Danes understand this: light is the ultimate luxury.

Lofty Heights

Once upon a time, when a rough, nameless neighbourhood of Lower Manhattan was dark and empty and only remarkable for its darkness and emptiness, Giorgio Deluca opened a cheese store on Prince Street, a pioneering business selling speciality Italian provisions to other brave pioneers who had stumbled into the area. The rest, as they say, is history. But for those who have been sleeping under a rock for several decades, he went on to open the legendary food emporium Dean & Deluca with partner Joel Dean, then a much-needed local resource but more recently a retail magnet for tourists.

Of course, nowadays those early settlers are entitled to feel rather smug as they rattle around the enormous lofts they bought for a song back in the day – after all, they invented SoHo, loft living, the whole Downtown NYC cliché.

OPPOSITE As you might expect, Giorgio Deluca's kitchen is as extensively equipped as any professional one. Open to the whole lower floor, it is concentrated around a wall of windows that look over the rooftops of Lower Manhattan. A vast cast-concrete island divides the space from the living area.

THIS PAGE In the dining area, three terracotta bowls found in Italy line up on a console table.

The living area of the loft is accessed directly from an elevator that opens into the space. Different zones are arranged in the vicinity of several large banks of windows; a white leather Corbusier chaise teamed with two long, low sofas and a glass-topped coffee table serve as a sitting area. The sculptural cantilevered staircase visually divides the kitchen zone from the living room and leads to a rooftop bedroom, a garden and bathroom.

Today, the bankers and hedge fund folk are the only ones who can afford the neighbourhood, and SoHo is positively awash with chain stores and cappuccinos. Giorgio Deluca, undoubtedly a man of singular vision, renovated a raw industrial space into a vast penthouse duplex, complete with a roof garden fit for an empire builder.

An elevator to the penthouse opens directly onto the open-plan first floor, huge enough to cycle or rollerskate around, perfect for parties and hanging around the super-sized kitchen island sampling wine from the state-of-the-art temperature-controlled wine storage that runs along one wall.

One wall of the loft is devoted to Vitsoe metal shelves arranged with meticulous rows of books and vinyl records stationed next to a desk. There's a collection of guitars and instruments on stands opposite this library area.

The floor plan allows for several distinct zones: a sitting area made for congregating around a symmetrical arrangement of two vast white sofas and a pristine Mies van der Rohe leather day bed; a little further over there's an office area stationed opposite Vitsoe shelving laden with books, records and CDs, and a long dining table occupies an area opposite large factory windows.

Classic is the word that comes to mind to describe the interior's style. The sculptural black Cherner side chairs, Bertoia bar stools

and lighting by Artemide, a cherrywood, glass and sandblasted aluminium kitchen equipped with every item in a chef's *batterie de cuisine*, a poured concrete floor, a floating concrete staircase; restrained and functional (yet not utilitarian), these timeless, monochromatic contents define loft style at its purest. Giorgio Deluca might have the luxury of space, but he seems to feel not the slightest compulsion to fill it with too much stuff or to flirt with design fads, let alone the merest hint of colour.

OPPOSITE In the spirit of 1990s minimalism, the loft room is plain and functional, with a bed sporting crisp white linens, a headboard integrating Italian reading lamps to either side and an Eames Lounge chair and ottoman.

ABOVE A freestanding claw-foot bathtub sits in the middle of the large bathroom. The pitched roofline, round window and traditional tub give the room unexpected character.

Neutral Territory

Architects seem to have an ambiguous relationship with colour, preferring to deal with form, function and texture over decoration. Partners in life and work, Stefanie Brechbuehler and Robert Highsmith of architectural firm Workstead will happily admit that they are no exception. When Indian clients accustomed to bright colours sheepishly asked them to add some to their interior scheme, they suggested integrating brass details rather than use any paint shade other than a neutral.

Naturally, when they found their own home, a 'parlor floor' apartment in a Brooklyn brownstone painted blue, pink and yellow, their first instinct was to wash the whole thing in white emulsion. Given that the space is really three main rooms that flow into each other, limiting the colour palette made perfect sense; the two sets of dividing doors are often left open, creating a view all the way through from the street elevation to the garden at the back.

LEFT An angular, L-shaped linen sofa in the living area takes up a large amount of the room's real estate. Stefanie and Robert have recently added one of their own designs: the Sling chair (an updated version of the Safari chair designed by Kaare Klint) with a pivoting leather back and seat, paired with a footstool.

LEFT Robert's inherited glossy black lacquer piano is both a functional element and a decorative sculptural object, complementing the regulation colour scheme and asymmetrical arrangement of framed monochrome illustrations. An adjustable Workstead signature lighting fixture is attached to the wall.

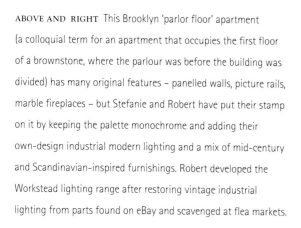

ABOVE AND RIGHT This Brooklyn 'parlor floor' apartment
(a colloquial term for an apartment that occupies the first floor
of a brownstone, where the parlour was before the building was
divided) has many original features – panelled walls, picture rails,
marble fireplaces – but Stefanie and Robert have put their stamp
on it by keeping the palette monochrome and adding their
own-design industrial modern lighting and a mix of mid-century
and Scandinavian-inspired furnishings. Robert developed the
Workstead lighting range after restoring vintage industrial
lighting from parts found on eBay and scavenged at flea markets.

While the Workstead partners relish the 19th-century vernacular details – mouldings, pocket doors, high ceilings, sash windows and two marble fireplaces – they have relied on a few Scandinavian Modern and mid-century pieces to update the look and feel of the interior to something that feels younger and hipper. There are dining chairs by Eames and Nelson, collections of found objects, abstract paintings and prints and their own sculptural lighting designs, inspired by vintage industrial elements. Favourite materials, a combination of wood, leather and linen, add a layer of warmth to the look, functioning as the team's substitute for colour or pattern.

Robert's taste for Scandinavian design has its roots in his upbringing. His architect grandfather and painter grandmother filled their house with classic mid-century designs, which he inherited while still at art school (apparently resulting in a precociously stylish dorm room). An immersion in this aesthetic informs the partners' approach to creating their own products, which ensure that they can always stamp their signature look on future projects. They recently invented their own version of the Safari chair, which comes in leather or canvas combined with a cherry, oak or walnut structure.

Despite a predilection for the quieter side of the colour wheel, Stefanie and Robert have dared to experiment with Farrow & Ball's Hague Blue at the Wythe Hotel's Ides bar, and secretly look forward to persuasive clients with other ideas.

LEFT The third space at the back of the apartment, overlooking the garden and next to a tiny white kitchen, is used as a dining room and study area with a small vintage desk. Robert inherited the set of Paul McCobb spindle-back chairs from his architect grandfather and painter grandmother. A Workstead Industrial Chandelier hangs over the dining table.

ABOVE AND LEFT Postcards from Robert and Stefanie's long-distance courtship fit neatly into a vertical space. A metal office locker (left) is an ideal spot for the bar.

OPPOSITE Brownstones have elongated floor plans that include small rooms in the mid-section that rarely see much daylight, making them ideal for use as bedrooms. Robert and Stefanie have kept the room very spartan, with just a bed flanked by two lamps of their own design.

THIS PAGE AND RIGHT A combined white kitchen/dining room has a utilitarian feel, with a stainless-steel extraction hood and fitted oven. A waist-height white wall conceals the guts of the kitchen when viewed from the dining room side of the room. Claus made the long reclaimed plank and metal table especially for the space, where the couple spends a lot of time entertaining friends.

The New Black

Living right in the heart of a city is usually a privilege reserved for Russian oligarchs, oil barons, rock stars and their kin, but it is reassuring that in some capitals it's still possible for the creative classes to stake their claim to a prime patch of inner-city real estate. Ingeborg Wolf, fashion stylist and sometime designer, and her partner Claus Larsen, a furniture designer/maker/retailer, were lucky enough to find a flat in the centre of Copenhagen in an old office building that now combines residential living with business premises, and two years after first spotting it, they were able to snag it as their own.

Originally a showroom for fashion brands, the open-plan space with high ceilings, concrete floors and lots of windows seemed to be an ideal blank canvas that they could adapt to meet their particular needs by making some simple but effective structural changes. Adding a partially glazed dividing wall in the living room created a large visible storage area for Ingeborg's impressive wardrobe of clothes hung on metal rails in the manner of a boutique (echoing the apartment's past life).

The living room with its liquorice black floor and white panelled walls has just a few dramatic pieces to establish a 'look': the chain chandelier hung low in the corner and an expansive modular sofa made by Claus. Concrete plinths display sculptural black objects and a vase of acid green blooms.

HELMUT NEWTON

CHANE

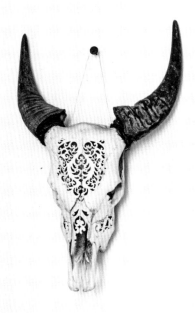

Custom-built shelves are laden with monochrome objects, fashion monographs, magazines and books of black and white photography. The intricately carved skull is the one decorative object in the space. A fringed bag hangs from a folded metal chair.

THIS PAGE Deep shelves are heaped with neatly folded clothes, heels, boots and boxes of accessories. Ingeborg's open-to-view wardrobe requires strict discipline to maintain order.

OPPOSITE Ingeborg inherited the taxidermied snow owl from her grandfather, and the Rick Owens-designed vessels were a present from Claus. The surfboard makes the edit as it is the right colour: black, naturally.

The monochrome colours and textures glimpsed through that glazed screen further establish the sartorial theme; Ingeborg's metier has become a decorative motif throughout, with an enviable parade of shoes, accessories and black and white fashion monographs showcased on open shelves in the living room. The colour scheme may be extreme, but furniture and materials in contrasting textures help keep things interesting; iron, wood, concrete, glass and rusted chain all contribute to the rough luxe mix. Ingeborg spotted the chandelier in a shop window before she had a high enough ceiling to fix it to, and dreams of living in a ruined castle with two of them suspended over a long table.

OPPOSITE AND RIGHT Glazed black metal screens divide the space into separate zones without compromising the available daylight. They stop below the decorative coving, allowing a new architectural element to juxtapose with the old. In the living room, Ingeborg has carved out a space for her desk where she sits at an angular metal grid chair softened by a longhaired black sheepskin. Towering piles of magazines are neatly stored in rows against the wall. Behind the glass screen you can glimpse her well-ordered double-height hanging rails of clothes, a reminder of the apartment's former life as fashion showroom (right).

PAGES 184–185 Painted black, the minimal bedroom reverses the balance of light and dark. A simple shelf behind the bed functions as a headboard and somewhere to rest personal mementos like the bird's feather in a vase and black and white framed photos. A glass laboratory vessel rests on a vintage tripod.

They wanted to find a sofa long enough for both of them to stretch out on, so Claus made one exactly the right size, as he did the dining table in the white-on-white kitchen/dining room where they spend most of their free time.

Although the modish look of the interior springs from a 'fashion' sensibility, the careful selection of objects and furnishings is not without sentiment. Taxidermy, yes, mirrored furniture, check, but both the snow owl and a mirrored table are family heirlooms that trigger memories.

Choosing monochrome is a reflex for Ingeborg, who sees the palette as a calming one after hectic days of 'visual noise' styling fashion videos. She cites Parisian ateliers as an influence, particularly that of Rick Owens, the reigning king of minimalist Goth glamour. Working from a home office on one side of the living room means that she must keep a sense of order at all times, so a tightly edited selection of possessions is essential. And glass walls require domestic discipline; the bed must always be made.

Sources UK

Appley Hoare Antiques
9 Langton Street
London SW10 0JL
+44 (0)20 7351 5206
appley@appleyhoare.com
*Specializing in 18th- and
19th-century French
country antiques.*

Blott Kerr Wilson
blottsshellhouses.com
*Shell artist who makes
extraordinary rooms or wall
art with shells.*

Butler's Emporium
70–71 George Street
Hastings
East Sussex TN34 3EE
+44 (0)1424 430678
*Vintage furniture, home
accessories, tablewares, art.*

Baileys Home
and Garden
Whitecross Farm
Bridstow
Herefordshire HR9 6JU
+ 44 (0)1989 561931
baileyshome.com
*Salvaged furniture and
utilitarian kitchenware.*

Caravan
5 Ravenscroft Street,
London E2 7SH
+44 (0)20 7033 3532
caravanstyle.com
By appointment only.
*Unique selection of quirky
vintage and vintage-inspired
decorative items.*

Igigi
34a Western Road
Hove
East Sussex BN3 1AF
+44 (0)1273 775257
igigigeneralstore.com
*Distinctive furniture,
homewares and accessories
with a European feel.*

Lassco
Brunswick House
30 Wandsworth Road
London SW8 2LG
+44 (0)20 7501 7775
lassco.co.uk
Architectural salvage.

Ochre
46–47 Britton Street
London EC1M 5UJ
+ 44 (0)20 7096 7372
ochre.net
*Purveyors of contemporary
upholstery, lighting, mirrors
and accessories. Visit their
website for details of their
NYC showroom.*

Pimpernel & Partners
596 Kings Road
London SW6 2DX
pimperneelandpartners.co.uk
+44 (0)20 7731 2448
*Antique furniture, replica
French chairs and decorative
accessories for the home.*

Retrouvius
1016 Harrow Rd
London NW10 5NS
+44 (0)20 8960 6060
retrouvious.com
*Architectural salvage and
accessories.*

Josephine Ryan
17 Langton Street
London SW10 0JL
+44 (0)20 7352 5618
josephineryan.co.uk
*Antique furniture, textiles,
lighting, tableware and mirrors.*

Trouver Antiques
59 South Hill Park
London NW3 2SS
+44 (0)7973 885671
trouverantiques.co.uk
*Decorative industrial French
and English furniture.*

Warp & Weft
68a George Street
Hastings
East Sussex TN34 3EE
+44 (0)1424 437 180
www.warpandweftstyling.com
*Leida Nassir-Pour's vintage
clothing store. She also has her
own clothes label inspired by
vintage pieces.*

MARKETS AND
ANTIQUE FAIRS

Ardingly
International Antique and
Collectors Fairs
+44 (0)1636 702 326
iacf.co.ukInternational
*Antiques and collectors' fair,
held several times a year.*

Camden Passage Market
Islington
London N1 5ED
camdenpassageislington.co.uk
Vintage clothing and homewares.

Goodwood Racecourse
antique and collectors fair
Goodwood Racecourse
Chichester
West Sussex PO18 0PX
*The largest antiques and
collectors fair in West Sussex
boasting 300 stalls.*

Sunbury Antiques Market
at Kempton Park
www.sunburyantiques.com
*Britain's largest antiques and
collectors fairs, held twice
monthly.*

Sources US

ABC Carpet & Home
888 & 881 Broadway
New York, NY 10003
+1 (212) 473 3000
abchome.com
*A carefully chosen,
continuously evolving
assortment of furniture,
antiques, textiles and
accessories from around
the world.*

Anthropologie
anthropologie.com
*Bright, Bohemian, eccentric
accessories, tableware and
furniture.*

Beall & Bell
430 Main St, Greenport
New York, NY 11944
+1 (631) 477 8239
beallandbell.com
*Vintage furniture, lighting
and accessories.*

Cafiero Select
36 East 2nd Street
New York, NY 10003
+1 (212) 414 8821
*Interior designer, David
Cafiero's colourful, chic vintage
and antiques emporium.*

Canvas
123 West 17th Street
New York, NY 10011
+1 (212) 372 7706
and at
199 Lafayette Street
New York, NY 10012
+1 (646) 873 6698
canvashomestore.com
*Great tableware, upholstery
and accessories.*

John Derian
6 East Second Street
(between 2nd Avenue and
the Bowery)
New York, NY 10003
+1 (212) 677 3917
johnderian.com
*Fine linens, textiles, furniture,
art and accessories.*

Dwell Studios
77 Wooster Street
New York, NY 10012
+1 (646) 442 6000
dwellstudio.com
*Mid century modern style and
vintage furniture, lighting and
accessories.*

Home Stories
148 Montague Street
Brooklyn, NY 11201
+1 (718) 855 7575
www.homestories.com
*A newcomer to NYC, this
store is devoted to monochrome
furniture, linens and lighting
with a distinctly European feel.*

Olde Good Things
Union Square
5 East 16th Street
New York, NY 10003
+1 (212) 989 8814
Architectural antiques.

Restoration Hardware
restorationhardware.com
*Reproduction furniture,
hardware and linens.*

Terrain
561 Post Road East
Westport, CT 06880
+1 (203) 226 2750
shopterrain.com
*Outdoor-themed merchandise
from Anthropologie.*

Michele Varian
27 Howard Street
New York, NY 10013
+1 (212) 343 0033
michelevarian.com
*Independent retail at its best –
eclectic furniture, tableware,
accessories, lighting, wallpapers
and fabric.*

FLEA MARKETS

**Brimfield Antique Show
Massachussetts**
For dates and directions,
visit brimfieldshow.com
*Huge market held three times
a year.*

**Original Round Top
Antiques Fair**
Texas
For dates and directions,
visit www.roundtoptexas
antiques.com
*Enormous flea market full of
treasures.*

Rose Bowl flea market
Pasadena, California
For dates and directions,
visit rgcshows.com
*On the second Sunday of each
month.*

Sources Europe

Caravane
19 rue Saint Nicolas
75012 Paris
France
+33 1 53 02 96 96
caravane.fr
*Excellent interiors store
with eponymous range of
upholstered furniture,
linens and accessories.*

Emery et Cie
78 Quai des Charbonnages
1080 Brussels
Belgium
+32 2 513 58 92
emeryetcie.com
Wallpapers, furniture, paints.

Granit
Götgatan 31
116 21 Stockholm
Sweden
+46 8 642 10 68
www.granit.com
*Inexpensive but stylish
Scandinavian design store
selling monochrome home
goods and clothes.*

Hay
Pilestraede 29-31
1112 Copenhagen K
Denmark
+45 42 820 820
www.hay.dk
*Innovative but classic design
store with merchandise inspired
by Danish Modern designs.
There are stores throughout
Europe and their first UK store
has just opened in Bath.*

Lily Oscar
Lerbergsvägen 37
263 32 Höganäs
Sweden
www.lilyoscar.com
*Charming store housed in
owner's garage selling a
monochrome mix of furniture
and accessories.*

Lotta Agaton Shop
Rådmansgatan 7, BV
S-114 25 Stockholm
Sweden
www.lottaagaton.se
*The eponymous home goods
store of Sweden's celebrated
stylist. Open Thursdays only.*

Maison HAND
11bis rue Jarente
69002 Lyon
France
+33 4 78 37 05 92
*Monochrome heaven! The
South of France's chicest
interiors emporium.*

Spazio Rossana Orlandi
Via Matteo Bandello 14-16
20123 Milano
Italy
+39 02 467 4471
www.rossanaorlandi.com
*Beautifully merchandized
vintage and contemporary
furniture store in an ancient
building in Milan.*

Studio Oliver Gustav
Store Strandstraede 9
1255 Copenhagen
Denmark
+45 27 374 630
olivergustav.com
*A boutique focused on
monochrome furniture,
antiques and objects both
antique and contemporary.*

Picture Credits

1 The home of Giorgio DeLuca in New York; 2 The home of the architect Joseph Dirand in Paris; 3 left The home of Marie Worsaae of Aiayu; 3 centre The home of designer and stylist Annaleena Leino Karlsson in Stockholm; 3 right and 4 The home of the architect Jonas Bjerre-Poulsen of NORM Architects; 5 Workstead; 6 The home of Marzio Cavanna in Milan; 7 left Dr Parashkev Nachev's studio; 7 right The home of Marzio Cavanna in Milan; 8–9 The home of Giorgio DeLuca in New York; 10–11 Designed by Stéphane Garotin and Pierre Emmanuel Martin of Maison Hand in Lyon; 11 right The London home of Adriana Natcheva; 12–35 Still-lifes styled by Hilary Robertson; 36–39 The home of the architect Jonas Bjerre-Poulsen of NORM Architects; 40 The home of the architect Joseph Dirand in Paris; 41 left The home of Marie Worsaae of Aiayu; 41 right The home of the architect Jonas Bjerre-Poulsen of NORM Architects; 42 The home of Marie Worsaae of Aiayu; 43 The home of designer and stylist Annaleena Leino Karlsson in Stockholm; 44–45 The home of the architect Joseph Dirand in Paris; 46–47 The London home of Adriana Natcheva; 48 Designed by Stéphane Garotin and Pierre Emmanuel Martin of Maison Hand in Lyon; 49 The home of the stylist Ingeborg Wolf; 50–51 The home of Marzio Cavanna in Milan; 52 left The home of the architect Jonas Bjerre-Poulsen of NORM Architects; 52 right The London home of Adriana Natcheva; 53–55 Designed by Stéphane Garotin and Pierre Emmanuel Martin of Maison Hand in Lyon; 56 The home of Marzio Cavanna in Milan; 58–67 The home of designer and stylist Annaleena Leino Karlsson in Stockholm.; 68–79 The home of Marzio Cavanna in Milan; 80–89 The home of the architect Joseph Dirand in Paris; 90–101 Designed by Stéphane Garotin and Pierre Emmanuel Martin of Maison Hand in Lyon; 102–111 Summerhouse on Furillen, Gotland by Imberg Arkitekter, www.imbergarkitekter.se; 112–121 The family home of the architect Johan Israelson on Gotland www.iaa.nu; 122–129 Naja Munthe, owner of MUNTHE in Copenhagen; 130–137 Dr Parashkev Nachev's studio; 138–147 The home of the architect Jonas Bjerre-Poulsen of NORM Architects; 148–155 The home of Marie Worsaae of Aiayu; 156–163 The home of Giorgio DeLuca in New York; 164–173 Workstead; 174–185 The home of the stylist Ingeborg Wolf.

Business Credits

Aiayu

Dampfaergevej 2A

2100 Copenhagen

Denmark

+45 33 32 32 80

E: mw@aiayu.com
www.aiayu.com

Pages 3 left, 41 left, 42,
148–155.

Annaleena Leino
Karlsson

Sånga-säbyvägen 178

17996 Svartsjö

Sweden

+46 (0)73 600 46 26

E: info@annaleena.se
www.annaleena.se

Pages 3 centre, 43, 58–67.

Israelson/Andreini
Arkitektur

Birger Jarisgatan 62

114 29 Stockholm

Sweden

www.iaa.nu

Pages 112–121.

Marzio Cavanna and
Cristiana Giva
Architects

MC2 Studio

www.mc2studio.com

Pages 6, 7 right, 50–51, 56,
68–79.

Joseph Dirand
Architecture

51 rue Saint Georges

75009 Paris

France

+33 (0)1 44 69 04 80

E: jd@josephdirand.com
www.josephdirand.com

Pages 2, 40, 44–45, 80–89.

Imberg Arkitekter

Pröstgatean 62

111 29 Stockholm

Sweden

+46 (0)707 356 601

www.imbergarkitekter.se

Pages 102–111.

Ingeborg Wolf

www.ingeborgwolf.dk

and

Oliver Gustav Studio

www.olivergustav.com

and

Clarrods

www.clarrods.com

Pages 49, 174–185.

Maison Hand

11bis rue Jarente

69002 Lyon

+ 33 (0)4 78 37 05 92

E: info@maison-hand.fr
www.maison-hand.com

Pages 10–11, 48, 53–55,
90–101.

MUNTHE

www.munthe.com

Pages 122–129.

Adriana Natcheva
Groves Natcheva
Architects

6 Kensington Mews

London W8 5DR

+44 (0)20 7937 7772

E:info@grovesnatcheva.com
www.grovesnatcheva.com

Pages 7 left, 11 right, 46–47,
52 right, 130–137.

Jonas Bjerre-Poulsen
NORM Architects

Snaregade 14

1205 Copenhagen

Denmark

E: info@normcph.com
www.normcph.com

Pages 3 right, 4, 36–39, 41
right, 52 left, 138–147.

Workstead

The Old American Can
Factory

232 Third Street E102

Brooklyn

NY 11215

+1 (347) 689 2766

E: info@workstead.com
www.workstead.com

Pages 5, 164–173.

Index

Page numbers in *italic* refer to the captions

Acknowledgments

Almost two years ago, I started a board on Pinterest named Monochrome after finding so many inspiring pictures on the web; on Scandinavian blogs like emmas.blogg.se and stilinspiration.blogspot.se and in Scandinavian magazines *Rum* and *Residence*. I knew that there was a new story to tell. There have always been monochrome interiors, but the homes I was finding had a fresh look that I was keen to dissect.

Thank you to the team at RPS for seeing the potential in that story; to Annabel, Cindy, Leslie and Jess for all their help turning an idea into a book. The deadline always seems like a very far-off point on the horizon, and then suddenly momentum is required. Thanks to Annabel, flatplan wizard and editor, I managed to enjoy writing the book despite my laptop's demise. Photographer Pia Ulin took the most wonderful pictures and was a dream companion on our European tours. I always admire a light packer!

Designer Paul Tilby, thank you for your clean, understated design approach, which allows the pictures to tell the story. And a huge thank you to the trusting home owners who allowed us to shoot their spaces, sometimes without even meeting us. When I can't meet the people who inhabit these homes, I enjoy imagining them after spending time with their possessions, rather like a reader of this book.